CONSUMING
The Kitchen Poems

St. Louis   1980s

poems by

Charlotte McCaffrey

Finishing Line Press
Georgetown, Kentucky

For women in kitchens everywhere.
And for Phyllis, my last—and best—customer.

Some of this is true. None of it is false.
—The Old Chef

ACKNOWLEDGMENTS

With thanks and gratitude to the Mini Buddha Pumpkin group of 2020

Publisher: Leah Huete de Maines
Editor: Christen Kincaid
Cover Art: vectorfusionart/shutterstock.com
Author Photo: Phyllis Hoffman
Cover Design: Elizabeth Maines McCleavy

Order online: www.finishinglinepress.com
also available on amazon.com

Author inquiries and mail orders:
Finishing Line Press
PO Box 1626
Georgetown, Kentucky 40324
USA

Contents

AN ORDER OF CHAOS

We create chaos
from the order of nature.

We wrench the greens
and carrots from the earth
scatter them
on chilled china plates
crack the eggs
disjoint the chicken
butcher the cow and pig.

We create order
from the chaos of nature.

We emboss the mushrooms.
Carve the tomatoes into roses.
Whip the eggs
into frothy peaks of meringue.
Top the just-crisped leg
of a lamb
with a tiny frilled white hat.

We break it all up.
We make it all up
as we go.

EGGS

One case:
five flats of thirty-six count.
Fifteen dozen.
One hundred and eighty eggs.

Just the start
on a Sunday morning.

We heat them, beat them, whip them
temper them with warm butter.

Spread our fingers
gently hold the yolk
let the glair slip through.

A little attention
they'll do almost anything.
Accommodating to every meal.

Benedict (eggs on eggs!)
souffles, sauces
mousse and meringue.
Divinity.

Labor and delivery of the lady birds.
Oeuf—ironically—a masculine noun in French.

Caviar of the barnyard.
So much depends
upon the white chickens.

Eggs. The start of it all.

BIRD

He's a heavy man
an easy 250 and not very tall.
Married to a woman
who has a twin sister.
Sometimes it's like I got two,
he says. *But I only wanted one.*
The sister and his wife so close.
*I don't know what they talk about
but she comes home mad at me.*

He sings softly when
it's slow. Mostly church songs
or a little R and B.
Bird.

He's a good dishwasher.
Doesn't hold us cooks up
like some do—
the food ready and no plates.
He gets the busboys
what they need too
as fast as he can.
Bird is on time.

He doesn't drink the leftover booze
that comes back in the dirty glasses—
what the other dishwashers save
and chug later
calling it Jungle Juice.
He's sober and clean.

One Sunday brunch we got slammed
with orders for our signature
banana pecan waffles.
Syrup was getting low.
Chef sent Bird to the store
on a quick trip to get more.
Get the Karo brand, he told him
(He was a cheap chef).
Bird's face a blank.

Oh, right, said chef. *I forgot.*
He handed him an empty bottle.
Take this.
Even so, Bird brought back
the wrong kind—
light instead of dark.
Chef's mouth so tight
waitresses complaining.

So he sent a busboy
the one working just for the summer
Yale in the fall.
The one who called out to Bird
(but only once)
Cutlery!
when he needed knives and forks.
Napery!
for the linens.

All of us laughing at college boy.
Bird just trying to figure out
what in the world he wanted.

Anthony.

CRIMSON FANCIES

The farmer's market—
worth a trip for the tomatoes alone.
Purveyors sometimes deliver
those hothouse numbers
to the restaurant:
muscular, firm as tennis balls
or silicone implants.
They just won't do.

At the market
I look for Crimson Fancies
or nice Early Girls.
So fragrant that
a perfume
could be pressed from them
dabbed on pulse points.
Fat ruby rounds
that a few hours earlier
were swelling
from their snaky vines.

I ask the farmer
how he grows such beauties.
Steady heat, he says.
And I water

regularly
thoroughly
deeply
slowly.

BOUREE

We dance
in a workshop
of flesh and bones:
liver and legs
breasts and beef.

With cream and yeast
butter and eggs
vegetables, fruit
grains and roots.

Our tools are also
flesh and bones:
hands, noses
tongues.

Joined with pans
pots, and tongs
knives and flames
china cap strainers.

We score, we call and check.
We whip and twist and stuff.

Surrounded
by sounds, smells, and tastes
we go by the book.
We cook.

Whatever you order.
Whatever we can do.
We dance the dance.
We do.

THE OLD CHEF I
Or The Corpulent Coxswain

He churns
through the kitchen
bloated   fat   slow
his white jacket a sail
toque a mast
as if he were
not only the coxswain
but the ship itself.
Everyone moves out of his way.

He looks at the reservation book.
Holds a bouquet of silver spoons
to taste the morning's work.
He wants to correct the seasoning
but at this age his taste buds are dull.
Old chefs tend to oversalt
trying to bring up
the flavors they remember
from the past.
He needs his sous chef
to follow behind
double check him.

He yells
at the woman working the pantry
whose name he calls out
like a curse.
This lettuce isn't crisp.
Did you wash it in ice water?

He screams
at the waiters
if they are slow picking up
the dishwasher to bring
more ten-inch liners
monkey dishes
for sauce on the side.
He commands from his helm
when the rush begins
snatches tickets from the spindle

barks them out to the line
gives the cooks an "all-day"—
a recap of our orders—
when we need one.

He watches
non-stop motion
the blur
that is us
straining
in sync
at the broiler
the grill
the fryer
the sauté stations
doing what he no longer
has to do
what he can't do
even if he wants to.

DOG

Dog preps the shrimp and lettuce
bakes off the house bread
carries the heavy trays to the waiters
in the upstairs dining rooms.
He sometimes calls out
as he weaves through us
Lady with a baby! Out the way!
or
Greyhound! Coming through!

For that, and because
he's whippet thin and fast
he gets called Dog.

Snarling sometimes
smiling others.
Never drops
so much as a fork.

Lorenzo.

THE REGULARS

The waiter yells *Crazy Bob on fourteen*
when he brings in the order.
The ticket is marked CB in big letters.
Bob, a very short man, has heavily oiled brown hair
with a sharp military part.
Chunky gold pinky ring
smokes Swisher Sweets.
Always orders a double
stuffed shrimp appetizer as an entrée.
Sends it back in a flash—
Not hot enough! —
if he's with a new date.
Rumor has it he lives
with his mother.
Laughs so loud, the other guests turn their heads.
Sits for hours, doesn't drink, lousy tipper.

Von Ceil comes in early every Friday evening.
Just her and a hardback book.
Silver hair pulled back in a bun
staidly dressed, solid colors, quiet jewelry.
Dry martinis. Don't fire her
medium rare steak until
she starts her second drink.
Isn't in a hurry, smiles at the staff
leisurely eats her dinner
and reads. Not sure
if that's her first name or her last.
Always pays cash, generous tipper.

The gossip columnist, Terry Burder
is in twice a month. Has the tight, surprised
look of someone who's had work done.
Scouts the dining rooms, chatting as he goes.
Asks his waiter, *Who's here?*
Keeps track of those he might mention
in tomorrow's paper.
Always seated at a good table.
Comes in the kitchen afterwards

likes to grab the asses
of the busboys and dishwashers.
The waiters are too old.
One night the pot washer
almost decked him with a sauté pan
but the owner quietly
ushered Terry out.
One word in his column
could ruin your business.
No one brought charges
not back then anyway.

Bob and Bill like a corner table
a little privacy
even in this haven where
their friends also dine.
They ask to sit
in Richard's section
say he's the best waiter.
Cocktails before, a shared dessert after.
When Bill died, one of the first
young men we lost
in the great plague of the 80s,
Bob came in less often
took a seat at the bar.
He said sitting alone at a bar
was different than
sitting alone at a table.
Sometimes he asked Richard
to bring him an appetizer
to have with his vodka gimlet
but he never stayed long.
Surprised many
when he lived to seventy-six.

THE OLD CHEF II
Or Kitchen Aria

He points to the onions
with the tip of his knife.
They are so cruel
he says.

The scrim of his nails
holds the white globe
fingers carefully retreating
as his blade approaches.

He could tell me—
his sous chef—
to do this task
but says he prefers
to stay in practice.

With no need
to watch his hands—
this task so familiar—
he can look at me
while he slices or chops them
minces them with garlic and mushrooms
for the duxelles
or rough cuts them with carrots
to go with the prime rib.

But the years
can't stem the streaming
tears that run
down his face.

Put on some Puccini
he says.
*There's no sense
wasting a good cry.*

THE KNIFE SHARPENER

A chef is only as good as his knives.
The Old Chef

The knife sharpener
arrives at the back door
like some medieval tinker.
Grizzled and bent
rough leather apron
that glints
with a glitter of metal.
His wagon sits outside.

He lays out a worn chamois
on our prep table
full of his own knives.
We'll use these
while he takes ours to grind.
Can't lose a minute.

His circuit takes him
to many back doors
so he brings news to our house:
who has a new sous chef;
whose business has slowed down;
the name of the Italian place
moving in down the block.

The men in the kitchen scowl
when they see him.
He burns off good steel
they groan. One moves his hand
near his crotch, glances at me
looks away. I stifle the smile
I feel coming on.

Watch your fingers, now.
You want to start and end with ten.
The knife sharpener's dull joke
repeated every time
as he lays our knives down.

I give him cash from the till.
Before leaving, he pauses
to hear what news
we might have for him.
I mention the owner's trip to France
the cook who walked out
eight o'clock on a Saturday night.
I make sure to name him.

And so, twice paid
he packs up gossip and gear
trundles off to the next back door.

CLOSE

Hour after hour I'm steeped
in blood and cream
handling the meat and sauces
the greens
almost everything
that will soon be on your plate.

My hands cut the filets
sauté the broccoli
macerate the berries
whip the sauces.

I check your order to see
that the vegetable is crisp
the meat a bit past rare
the garnish nestled just so.

Though we've never met
I know you
at Table 6
with three other people.
No appetizers, in a hurry
on your way to the theatre.

I've tasted
what you will soon taste
touched what will soon
be part of you.

Intimate stranger.

DUCK

Duck makes us all laugh.

Takes a slick salmon
he's about to clean
waves it back and forth
while chasing
the squeamish new busboy.

Before he filets a beef tenderloin
he holds it to the front of his pants
struts where he thinks
I can't see him.
You wish, says Lorenzo.

One day I catch him
crouched under a prep table
in the back of the kitchen.
What are you doing? I say.
More sheep than duck then
he looks up at me, mouth
sprinkled with crumbs.
Eating this fine pie you made.

I try to look mad.
Next time, just ask.

Donald. Of course.

APRIL'S ALLEY

A stream of asphalt runs behind
this restaurant's back door.
Iced in winter. Dormant.

By April, it begins
to break and teem.
Traffic flows again, moving past
the garbage bins and discards.
The month is announced
by ripe red berries
bright green asparagus
and hardy people
of the grocery cart brigade
with their rusted hulls
of private cargo.

A ragged regatta
moves down April's alley.

Stiff from their months
berthed in shelters
they squint at the sun
bow into the wind
make their regular stops:
this dumpster, that church
my back door.

I dole out sandwiches, oranges.
We chat about the weather
the problem of rats.
Then they push off
to sway and sway and sway
unanchored
toward May.

CONSUMING

Six a.m.
The kitchen shines.
Quiet, cool.
Every surface
clean and dry—
we leave it that way.
Tile, stainless, stove
the terracotta floors.
All of it glows.

The only aroma
is the first pot of coffee
just beginning to brew.

I check the books:
reservations
deliveries
schedules.
All in order.

Butter and flour started—
roux for the Bechamel.
A flat of eggs
is taken from the walk-in
to warm for meringues
the yolks saved
for Hollandaise, Bearnaise.

Ovens fired up
to roast bones
for the stock
then the prime rib, duck
the rack of lamb

to bake off the pies
the crusty house cheese bread.

The first prep cooks
arrive, chop the vegetables
clean the fish and the shrimp.

They sing and whistle
and joke and moan.

Some of them hungover
from their late-night partying.

Then begins the boiling
sputtering, sizzling
clang of metal on metal
staccato drum
of knives on the boards.

Clouds of steam
heat and sweat
100 degrees, then 110.
We're basting.
We soak
the linen napkins,
roll them up,
freeze them to wear—
icy neckerchiefs.

We bend into it
a heated race to be ready
for the Maître d's voice
calling out:
Doors are open! Showtime!

Then another race begins:
orders are shouted
over the din—
cooks yell
for sauté pans, plates.
Waiters call their tables.

The pot washer is high
the dishwasher late.
Then faster, even hotter.
Plateafterplateafterplate
the blur of it all, the high of it all,
nothing else but this
the work.

Consuming.

ONIONS

The deliveryman hoists
the red, netted sack to his shoulder
lugs it into the kitchen.
Fifty pounds, twice a week.

Not fancy, like asparagus
or passionate like tomatoes.
These are the peasantry
of the vegetables.

Pulled fresh from the dirt
they entertain and sustain us.
Lyonnaise us.

As essential as water and salt
we can't cook without them.
First scent from the stock pot
last to leave our hands and breath.

We've all had to peel them
chop them, suffer through them.

Myths are passed on
about the best way
to suppress the tears they cause:

Hold a matchstick
between your teeth like a toothpick.
Keep a piece of stale bread in your mouth.
Chill them first, rinse them first.
In summer, open the back door
and hope for a breeze.

One cook tried wearing a bandana
over his nose and mouth
while he diced them for soup.
Poor man looked like
a distraught robber
silver knife in hand
eyes pooled with tears.

None of it does any good.
A price the eyes must pay
for the pleasure of the tongue.

We have to have them.
They have to make us cry.

SHOWTIME!

We are performers
on this hot stage
costumed in white
moving to a range of notes.

We waltz to the
comforting bubble
of sauces and soups
tango to the
sizzle of garlic and onions
eggs in the sauté pan cackling.

A Buddy Rich jazzy percussion
of whisks and spoons
pans as they hit the burners
whoosh whoosh whoosh
of the dish machine.

Call and response:
Fire two tournedos, medium rare!
Yes, Chef!
Clean more shrimp!
Yes, Chef!
Sauté pans! Now!
Yes, Chef! Yes, Chef! Yes, Chef!

Waiters' rounds of complaint:
I called table 24—where is it?
Slap of plate coming back.
She says this steak is too rare.

Crescendo at the peak
of the rush
then a quieter hum
the softer strains
take us to closing
to the calming
Coda
at the bar next door.

RAT

He washes the pots and pans
does most of the cleanup
after closing—
the fryer, the floor
takes out the garbage.
Finishes up around two a.m.
too late to join us
next door.
A small man with furtive glances.
Sharp pinched face
moves quickly, says little
so the other guys call him Rat.
He doesn't seem to mind
intent on the business at hand.

When he stops showing up
for his shifts
I call and call but
there's no answer
then the line
is out of service.
Doesn't even come back
to pick up his last check.

Richard

HEIRLOOM TOMATOES
Or Tomatoes Redux

Centuries before they were catsuped
or salsaed or juiced or stewed;
ages before they appeared on the stage
with eggs as a vaudeville boo;
in that first garden
(of sticky choices)
a fruit for all seasons grew.

Nothing crisp spoiled
the bunch of us
and finally did us in.
That love apple
was a scalding
red tomato, full
of the pulp and seeds of sin.

Messy and dribbling
shamelessly staining
our damp collective skin.

THE OLD CHEF III
Or Presentation

Jacque's.
The fanciest French restaurant in the city.
Owned by the Belmondo brothers—
Jacques and Pierre.
(Real names: Jack and Pete.
They're actually Italian.)
An affable pair of restaurateurs
known to everyone
in the business.

Open on Monday nights
when my restaurant is closed
I go there with the old chef
who is now retired.

We anticipate investigating
the food as much as we do
the pleasure of eating it
dissecting each dish
to parse the flavors, ingredients.

First, escargot
the scent of garlic reaching us
before the plate does.
Each one ensconced in perfect shells
of flaky puff pastry.
Gastro-pods.

Cream of watercress soup. Consommé.
Steak au Poivre and cognac sauce.
Salmon Bearnaise.
Pommes Frites.
Lightly dressed greens
with curls of parmesan.

This is the 1980s.
This is haute cuisine.

We exchange plates with each other
then lean back, happily sated.

Jaques, a gracious host,
stops by our table
to see if we are happy.

Always glad to see you
he nods to the old chef
who introduces me.
He comps a dessert—
the gateau du jour—
a lovely chocolate confection.
We barely have room.

I ask for a tour of the kitchen.
Jacques leads us back
with obvious pride.
My mouth drops open.

Air conditioned
in the notorious heat
of this city.
Bright green ferns hang over
the line. Brass drain plates
shimmer in the floor.
We polish those, he says.

The only women I see
work in the pantry—
salads, cold appetizers.
Here, females are not allowed
on the line.

I'd love to work in this kitchen.
I tell the old chef as we walk out.
It's the very best.
He smiles at me
so ruefully, says
When onions are kind.

TOMCAT

Tomcat.
Sometimes Cat
or Koolcat.
Many names
for this dishwasher.
He's lean, tall
likes to wear sunglasses
even inside.
Not hard to guess why.
I don't push him
just say
Make sure you can see
that those dishes are clean.

Shortly after he quits
the police come around
want to know if we've seen him.
They tell us he is wanted for murder.

Years later, I read that he
has been tried and executed.
Oddly, the article online
reports his last meal:
shrimp and ice cream.

Thomas, we thought.
Vernon
we find out later.

SOFT SHELL CRABS

They arrive in slatted, wooden crates.
We hear rustling noises from inside
pry off a board, find them
nestled in wet straw.

Their shells
so cool
green and blue
I think of the water they came from
run my fingers quickly
over their slick, damp backs.

Before they are sautéed
the prep cook cleans them.
He snips away
the mouth and abdomen flap
pulls out their gills
rinses away the yellow ooze.
Their legs climb the air
then stop.

Once in the skillet
floured and seasoned
they blow up
like hot orange balloons
sputter and spit from the oil.
The line cook shakes the pan
but tries to keep his distance.

Same as frog legs.
he says.
They'll blister you bad.
They'll get you back.

MISS MARY

She is no longer young
doesn't miss those years.
One of fifteen children
her parents ushered in
to rural Arkansas.
Always just short of being full.
Just short of sleep, of room to stretch.
Three down from a new dress
eleven up from milk and a hip to ride on.
Unheard, unseen in the noise, the crowd.
Dull from lack, want, need.

Now she cleans the vast, empty
dining room of the restaurant.
She moves freely with rags, buckets
the vacuum cleaner.
She hums and talks out loud.

She says Jesus keeps her company,
they talk during the long hours.
We hear her from the kitchen
while we prep for dinner.
Her voice rises and falls
punctuated by pauses
then followed by murmurs
of agreement, sometimes laughter.

She works intently
in the open space.
Able at last to stretch
to enjoy the company
of one who can finally
pick her out from the rest.
This room her sanctuary
that sparkles and glows.

THE PRICE YOU PAY

First the feet.
The ache, the burning
that rest doesn't always ease.
A new kitchen means
breaking them into
a new floor.
Hard lessons those days.

The knees are next.
Beginning at age thirty
a low moan escapes from them
rises in decibels each year.

Sweaty rashes plague
the nether regions
raw and painful
after hours in 110-degree heat.
No one wants to mention this.

Arms striped, pockmarked
with cuts and burns.
You need a new safe word.
a friend jokes.

All of it worth the price.

Because the rush is the thing.
Not the dinner rush exactly
but the nightly flood
of adrenaline it brings.

The consuming work
that allows for nothing else
that numbs the pain
pushes out
all other thoughts
regrets worries bills
and broken hearts.

Always there.
Always needs me.
Holds me completely
in such rough, warm arms.

TURTLE SOUP

The meat gets shipped
frozen in rectangular blocks
shrink-wrapped in plastic
picture of a turtle on one side.
When thawed, it's picked through
to pull out the bones.

The first time anyone does this—
usually side work for the dishwasher
though we've all had to do it—
he stops to examine those
small white relics.

Turned this way and that
they look like crowns. Or wings.
Or the faces of lions and wolves.

I've seen those bones
slipped into pockets
taken home
painted gold or silver
then worn on chains around the necks
of some of the young cooks.
I've dried handfuls in the sun myself
arranged them on a windowsill.

After the meat is picked
we grind it, make the soup
and cook it all day—
it's a slow soup.

We serve it with a tiny glass
of sherry on the side
and it's very popular.
In the kitchen, though,
none of us will eat it.

LORENZO HAS HIS SAY

Let me tell you about this chef.

She is mean sometimes.
Says miss a Saturday night
you better bring me
your death certificate.

She makes me clean the lettuce
in ice water. The shrimp too.
Mince the garlic when
I have a date that night.

When the liquor started
to go missing, she had the
storeroom locks changed.
She screamed at all of us.
I don't think she knows
it was Tomcat—she might've
kicked his butt out the door.
We didn't say nothing
cause we don't mess with Tomcat.

But she'll lend you
ten dollars 'til payday.
Lets us go home early
if it's slow and we have plans
or maybe stay a little longer
if we need the hours.
One year, for Christmas she gave us
cash and a couple of joints.
And that time I cut my hand so bad
she wrapped it up
poured me a shot of Jack Daniels.

The last chef? He did people
in the prep kitchen
after we closed at night.
On the butcher block table.

Did blow too.
Kept a dollar and a razor blade
on salad plate
hidden behind a ceiling tile.
Everybody knew, and we knew
not to fool with it.

I had to work down there.
On that table. Every morning
scrubbing like crazy
before I started on the cheese bread.

She's not like that.

THE OLD CHEF IV
Or No Longer Serving

The restaurant years are long
behind me.
I only cook at home now.

Wash my own lettuce.
Chop my own onions.
Sharpen my knives.

I like simple, plain meals.
Salad. Soups. A good bread.

I don't miss the fourteen-hour days
the heat, the crazed pace
that was such a drug.

This cool room. This quiet life.

I putter in my small kitchen
some sweet music on in the background.
Leisurely stir the vegetable soup.
Season it to my own taste.

The salt shaker always close by.

Charlotte McCaffrey was born in Mobile, Alabama. As a child in a military family, she moved from California and Massachusetts to Maryland and Hawaii. She graduated from Washington University in St. Louis and then spent many years in the Midwest working as a chef. In 1989, she relocated to northern California where she worked as an elementary special education teacher for 25 years.

Her work includes the chapbook Reposed (Finishing Line Press) and has appeared in anthologies and journals, including *Bayou, The Comstock Review, Hampden-Sydney Poetry Review, MacGuffin, Poetry International, Sojourner, Women's Studies Quarterly*, and many others. Currently, she is retired and lives with her partner in the San Francisco Bay area where she writes, gardens, cooks, and dotes on her dogs.